Devotions for CHOIRS

Genevieve and Herman DeHoog

Abingdon Press

DEVOTIONS FOR CHOIRS
Genievieve and Herman DeHoog

Copyright © 1997 by Abingdon Press

This book is printed on acid free paper.

ISBN 0-687-052483

00 01 02 03 04 05 06 — 10 9 8 7 6 5 4 3

MANUFACTURED IN THE UNITED STATES OF AMERICA

Dedication

To the many choirs we have had the privilege of sharing
with in our ministry to the Lord. Our memories of our
friends and experiences are a great joy in our lives.

Doc and Genevieve

Contents

Will You be Ready?

Matthew 24:36-44

The thief on the cross was the topic in an adult Bible study I was sharing in several years ago. The wife of the pastor said she could not understand how Christ could accept the thief into heaven at the last minute. Too often there are those who are counting on Christ's acceptance at the last minute. Some try to figure out exactly when the day of Christ's return will be. Jesus tells us that we cannot know when, but must remain always ready for his return.

When I was a young girl, I always felt as if my mother could see and know everything I did. I know that thought often kept me from getting into trouble. As I gained understanding of Jesus as the Christ, my guiding force became his presence. I found myself asking Jesus for advice or trying to imagine how he would handle any given situation.

Through the years our responsibilities increase in relationship to our families, friends, co-workers, and fellow Christians. We can feel truly blessed in these relationships when we have Christ as the example and guiding force in all we do. Then we will be ready to meet the Lord face to face no matter when he returns.

At this season of Advent, let us put all our relationships in line with Christ's leading and make our hearts truly ready for his coming.

G.M.D.

prayer

We have come into your house O Lord, to serve you. May our service be not only with our lips but with our hearts in love for you and others. We thank you, God, that you have blessed us with your words to share with others through the language of the angels' music. Fill us with your Spirit to serve you always in your Son's name. Humbly we pray. Amen.

"Didn't Know Who He Was"

Matthew 3:1-12

The old Spiritual, *Sweet Little Jesus Boy,* speaks for many of us. It is often hard in our busy lives to take time to really know who Jesus Christ is.

John the baptizer was Jesus' cousin and yet he didn't realize that Jesus was the Messiah until He came to be baptized by John.

John spent his adult life trying to help people understand what it meant to change their whole way of living, and through repentance to be ready to meet and accept the Messiah. John was more than ready to meet the Messiah when Jesus came to be baptized at the river.

How often do we encounter religious people who seem to know everything about the Scriptures, but not how to love and care for those around them. They do not know who Christ really is.

Everyday we have many opportunities to help others to know the Messiah, but we can't help others to know Christ until we know and accept Christ in our hearts. To know Christ means letting Christ know the real you and allowing him to change you. It means letting go of our old life and turning around to follow Christ. To know Christ is to be in full relationship with him.

What a wonderful time of year to begin a new and meaningful relationship with the Christ who loves us.

G.M.D.

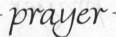

prayer

Gracious God, come and fill us with your Holy Spirit, that we may come to know you as you would have us know you. Help us to share your love in this season of love. We are so thankful that you love us as we are and forgive us when we fail. We pray we may be strong in your love, so that others may come to know you through us. In Jesus' name we pray. Amen.

Are You the Messiah?

Matthew 11:2-11

John's question from prison might be put to us as "are you a Christian?" Jesus' response was to say, "Look at what I am doing and what is happening all around me."

Our response might be similar. "Look at what we do." At Advent we see more of what it means to be a Christian than any other time of year. All of us seem to put our best foot forward in caring for shut-ins and those less fortunate than ourselves. We share with family and friends we seldom see, finding gifts or ways of showing people we love them. We prepare our best music, even though it means giving extra time from our busy schedules. All of these are ways of showing the love of Christ in us.

When we put our best self forward, we often sense the joy and peace that comes from giving and caring. Advent is a time of preparing ourselves for Christ's coming. May our best selves be the start of a new life for each of us. May we continue to always be ready for his coming so that others might always see his love in our lives.

G.M.D.

―――――――――― *prayer* ――――――――――

Great God of us all, just as John the Baptist led others to the Christ through his witness, may we lead others to Christ through our witness. You have blessed us with gifts of music. May we use our gifts in praise to you, that those who hear may find a newness in their faith and be drawn closer to you. In Christ's name and for his sake we pray. Amen.

Sing together: "I Want to Walk as a Child of the Light"

The Cost of Responding to God

Matthew 1:18-25

Has God spoken to you through dreams as he did to Joseph, or through angels as he did with Mary, or perhaps with music as he spoke to David? God is much more present in our lives than we ever want to admit. Or perhaps it is that if we acknowledge that presence, we feel we will have to submit to God.

As we come into Christmas week, let us listen more carefully to what God may be saying to us and consider what our response should be.

Joseph accepted God's command to take Mary for his wife, even though marrying a pregnant woman would surely mean his family and friends would reject him. God sent his Son as a gift to us knowing that he would be rejected, suffer, and even be put to death.

With Christmas only a few days away many of us are probably bemoaning the added expense of the season. There is no doubt that Americans *spend* too much, but can we really say we *give* too much? Perhaps the time spent preparing for extra music for the season has become a chore rather than a cause for rejoicing. If so, I urge you to consider the reason for our coming together. We've said it and sung it so often it has become old hat. But the wonder has not changed. God gave us the ultimate gift that first Christmas long ago. When we consider the sacrifice made to give us that incredible gift, our own gifts of time and money become very small indeed.

As we prepare for Christmas, let our hearts be open to the presence of God in our midst. May we rejoice in word, deed, and song for all that God has done for us.

G.M.D.

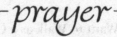 prayer

Sing together as a prayer: "My Soul Gives Glory to My God"

The Gift is Now

Luke 2:1-20

For me the high point of the Christmas season has always been sharing the birth of Christ in songs of praise on Christmas Eve. The choir becomes the angel choir to all those who come to share the service. Somehow the music takes on a heavenly sound on that night. Very often many of the choir members have colds or sore throats at this time of year, but God knows that many people await the sound of the choir proclaiming Christ's birth. So, sore throats or not, God uses the gifts given to us to produce the heavenly sounds to speak to those who will hear. Just as the angels sang to the shepherds, so we sing to God's people the glory of God's gift to all.

It took a special faith in God for Joseph and Mary to make the trip to Bethlehem when it was so close for her time to deliver. It took a special faith in God for the shepherds to respond to the message of the angels and then to share the message with anyone who would listen. It takes a special faith in God for us to share this same message with the people in our communities. It takes a special faith in God for those who hear the message to keep it in their hearts in the midst of this hurried season. What a wonderful thing God has done for us in the gift of his Son.

G.M.D.

prayer

Gracious and loving God, we thank you for the gift of your Son, Jesus Christ, and for giving us the privilege of telling others of your gift through our songs and Scriptures. You have truly blessed us and we pray our gift of music to you will bless others. We pray in your blessed Son's name. Amen.

SING: "There's a Song in the Air"

God With Us

John 1:1-4

Most of us who love to sing have found an opportunity to share in singing Handel's *Messiah*. The Scriptures are shared in exciting and majestic songs of the coming of the Messiah. Just as the prophets of old told the people over and over of the coming of one who would set them free from sin and death, so we continue to tell over and over of this same one; the Messiah, God with us, Wonderful, Counselor, the Mighty God.

What an overwhelming and awesome reality it is to know that Jesus the Christ is the ever present presence of God Almighty from the beginning, in the present, and for all eternity. The light of God in Christ shines for all peoples everywhere. We must never forget that this gift of Christ was given for any who accept and believe that Christ is the Son of God. When we hesitate to share the real meaning of Christmas for fear we might offend someone, we may be denying someone knowledge about the Son of God. At Christmas time, more people are open to hearing about Christ than almost any other time of year. Let us not miss an opportunity to share the joy and love of the Lord with those who don't know him now.

G.M.D.

prayer

Share together Psalm 98

SING: "He Is Born"

Through Suffering Comes Perfection

Hebrews 2:10-18

In our family, the weekend after Christmas is always our time of celebrating together and, therefore, a time to look forward to. For many, the week after Christmas can be a let down. Too often we feel relieved that Christmas is over, or perhaps our expectations were not fulfilled and we feel a sense of emptiness.

The writer of Hebrews wants us to understand that Jesus didn't just come as a sweet baby boy in a wonderful story, but that Jesus came to be one of us. Jesus came to share our joys and our sorrows, our highs and our lows. God took on human form in Jesus so that we might become true brothers and sisters in Christ. Just as we share the pains and joys of the members of our families, or the members of our choir, or church, or any group of close friends, so Jesus shares in our pains and joys as a part of our family.

Jesus willingly took on our sorrows and sufferings, even to the suffering on the cross for us. It was through his suffering that he completed the work necessary for our salvation and became perfection through fulfillment. Perfection in this context means completion and fulfillment. "Because he himself was tested by what he suffered, he is able to help those who are being tested" (Hebrews 2:18).

G.M.D.

prayer

Living God, help us understand all that Christmas truly means in the giving of your Son to become one of us. Help us to know that Christ is still willing to carry our sorrows and sufferings. If our hearts are lonely or sad, we know that Christ shares in our grief and eases our pain. If our hearts are joyful and full, we know Christ rejoices with us too. Thank you Lord, for always understanding. May we too become perfect in our suffering for you. In Christ's holy name. Amen.

A Time for New Beginnings

Revelation 21:1-6*a*

When I was young, I always tried to think of something to change in my life for my New Year's resolution. Usually they were things like, walk two miles every day, or eat less chocolate, or any number of things that pertained to my physical well being. As I became more enlightened to the needs of the world, my resolutions were more like, feeding the hungry or saving the children. The problem I always had was in carrying out my resolutions beyond the good intention stage.

John's vision of the new earth is not a new earth built on good intentions. The new year is a time for new beginnings for each of us through the power and guidance of the Holy Spirit.

God is the beginning and the end. God understands all things. If we want to know how to make realistic resolutions that can effectively make a new beginning in our lives, then we have to listen for the guidance of the Holy Spirit. New beginnings for God's world begin with persons reaching out and helping other people one person at a time.

Just as a magnificent chord of music is the building of one note upon another, so is God's world changed by helping one person and then another until a perfect harmony is created among the people of God.

G.M.D.

prayer

Here we stand Lord, at the beginning of a new year. May we use this year to share with your people in whatever way you lead us. Help us to be always open to your guidance that we may begin to create harmony not only in music, but in friendships and fellowships in our church, our homes, and our places of work. We pray always in Jesus' name. Amen.

SING: "O Morning Star, How Fair and Bright"

Where Are You Going?

Matthew 2:1-12

Not many of us in the Christian church are of Hebrew ancestry, so how grateful we should be for the Gentile wise men who came to worship Christ and open the doors for us to worship.

Once the wise men encountered Jesus as the Savior of the world, their lives were changed and they returned home a different way than they had come. I think they not only returned a different way physically, but also spiritually.

For many of us it is often hard to know in what direction the Lord is calling us to go. Sometimes it may mean physically moving from where we are to somewhere else that may be totally unknown to us. Abram left his home and went to a totally new land. He not only changed his location, but also his name. Joseph and Mary left and went to Egypt, and then returned to live in Nazareth. Jesus had no place to call his home once he began his public ministry. I sold most of my personal belongings and left my family to go 900 miles to a new place when God called me to serve. Although it has often been very difficult and at times scary, Christ's presence in the Holy Spirit has always shown me the way. Encountering Christ can often change our direction. Don't restrict your services for God to just one place but be ready to reach out wherever God sends you.

G.M.D.

 prayer

Lord, open our hearts and our minds so that we will be ready to go out for you in service. We are so grateful that you have given us an avenue by which to serve, now show us ways that we might expand our service for you through the power of your Holy Spirit. Amen.

SING: "If Thou But Suffer God to Guide Thee"

Acceptance Without Approval

Matthew 3:13-17

The choir in most churches is one place where everyone is welcome and accepted as a part of the whole group, whether they have a solo voice or just love to make a joyful noise to the Lord.

I have shared in a great many churches throughout my life, and I have been singing in choirs since I was twelve years old. The first and often closest friends in any new community has come from members of the choir, even when I was serving as a director of Christian education or as pastor. The bond that is made comes from a common love of singing praise to the Lord.

So it is in baptism. When we commit ourselves or renew the vows made for us in infant baptism, the Lord accepts us just where we are, and makes a relationship with us that lasts our whole life long. Even if we should stray away from Christ at some point in our lives, Christ is always ready and eager to accept us back.

When you reflect on the joy you share with those in your choir, think also of the joy of being a part of Christ's holy people through our common baptism with Jesus Christ and each other.

G.M.D.

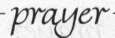

prayer

Sing together in an attitude of prayer, "Spirit of the Living God"

Witnessing for Christ

1 Corinthians 1:1-9

Paul puts a great deal of emphasis on spiritual gifts in much of his writings. In this greeting his emphasis includes using those gifts to witness for Christ.

Several years ago I began doing impersonations of women of faith. I was asked to do my Mary of Magdala for a group home of teenage youth. When I first appeared in costume the youth snickered and turned away. I went ahead and shared my story, putting the emphasis on how Christ changed me and gave me a new chance. In only about two or three minutes into my sharing, the young people began to listen more and more intently. When I finished the presentation, some of the youth asked me questions like, "Do you really know Jesus?" "Do you still live in Magdala?" "Did Jesus really change you?" It was very evident that Mary's story made an impression on several of them. What greater way to witness for Christ than using a gift you enjoy?

Both my ability to sing and to act are spiritual gifts given to me by the Holy Spirit. When I commit any performance to the Lord and seek the presence of the Holy Spirit, I know that the Lord will use my gifts to witness God's love to the people gathered.

Every Sunday as you gather to sing praises for the Lord as a part of the worship service, remember that the music you share is a gift of the Holy Spirit, given to you as a way to witness the love of the Lord in your heart.

G.M.D.

---
prayer

Gracious God, we thank you for the gifts of music that you have given to us. We pray that we may always use these gifts to witness your love to those who listen. Fill us with your Holy Spirit as we seek to share your word in Christ's name. Amen.

SING: "Spirit Song"

Called to Discipleship

Matthew 4:12-23

A few years back Doc and I had an opportunity to go to the Holy Land. When we first arrived in Tiberias, about 10 miles south of Capernaum, we looked out the window of our room which overlooked the Sea of Galilee and we were taken back to the time of Christ. The next morning we went out in a boat on the lake, heading up the coast line to Capernaum. We saw the little villages nestled in the hillsides and felt the presence of Christ all around us. We truly felt like disciples, wanting to know more and more. I almost expected to see the crowds gathering on the hillside to listen to Jesus.

We have been privileged to know Jesus through our many years of study of Scripture and work in the church, so it was easy for us to say "yes" to following Jesus. We know who he is. We know all that he did. We also know all he had to suffer to show his love for us. When he called those first disciples on the shores of Galilee, they did not know that Jesus was the light of the world sent by God. These fishermen knew Jesus as a great teacher, special friend to Peter and Andrew, and close cousin to James and John. They willingly left their life's work and families to go with Jesus and seek to understand all that he was about for God.

When Jesus calls us today to come and follow him, it still may be very hard to do. We are not all called to go out from our place of living to an unknown place, we can still follow Jesus where we are by sharing his love with others.

As members of the choir, we give not only our talents, but our time as well. Some days giving our time is very difficult. It is good always to remember the sacrifices of the early followers and of Christ himself.

G.M.D.

prayer

SING: "Lord You Have Come to the Lakeshore"

The Fuller Life

1 Corinthians 1:18-31

I have in my garden a wonderful old worn statue of Francis of Assisi holding a bird. A deer lies at his feet. The statue was given to me by a dear friend from her mother's precious belongings. I cherish the statue, but I admire more Saint Francis and the person he became.

As a young man he was wealthy, well educated, handsome, and lived life to the fullest, so he thought. One day he encountered Christ in a profound way that changed his life completely. He gave away everything he had to the poor and needy. He turned all his energy to serving Christ by humbly helping others far and wide and even helping the animals and birds. He saw all of God's creation, people and creatures, as blessings from God to care for. Then he truly understood what it meant to live life to the fullest.

Paul is trying to help us to realize that whoever we are and whatever we have are gifts to be used for Christ. Without the gifts God has given us, we are nothing. We must never see ourselves as better or wiser or more gifted than any other of God's children.

When the choir has worked hard on an anthem and the congregation shouts "amen" or claps, it is very easy for us to take the glory for that performance. It is important for us always to give the glory to God for all that we are able to do. Paul tells us that we must never boast in ourselves but only boast in Christ Jesus and give him the glory always.

G.M.D.

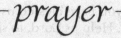

prayer

Share Psalm 15:1-5.

The Christian Flavor

Matthew 5:13-20

Begin your time today with singing together, "This Little Light of Mine."

This passage from Matthew makes me think of who we really are as a choir. We are the salt in the worship, or light shining in the midst of darkness.

When I was a child, one of my favorite desserts was my mother's chocolate pie. She was well known for her pies of any kind, but especially her chocolate pies. One Sunday our cousins came to visit and mother had made three chocolate pies for dessert. Her sister was in the kitchen talking to her while she was baking and she forgot a very important ingredient, not salt, but sugar. Did you ever try to eat a chocolate pie without any sugar in it? Impossible! Of course, we never let her forget about those pies.

We as Christians truly are the salt in the midst of a self-centered world. We are the light that can lead others out of the darkness of the secular world and into the light of God's world. What a responsibility. We cannot do it without the power and presence of the Holy Spirit.

As the choir we have a special responsibility to enhance the worship service with a very important flavor. We are the salt that brings the service together into a full harmony of thought and feeling in Christ's presence.

Many people choose a church because of the music that is a part of the service. It is part of our responsibility to help people grow in their "flavors" of music so that all "tastes" can feel the warmth of the light as shared by the choir.

G.M.D.

prayer

Wise and loving God, you have blessed us all in a very special way and we are truly grateful. Help us Lord, to share these blessings with your people in a way that may help them know you better. We come always as your humble servants, in Christ's name. Amen.

Growing with God

1 Corinthians 3:1-9

Sometimes I think that plants decide on their own if they are going to grow or not. I read the books, listen to friends, try to follow all the directions as carefully as possible, but sometimes things grow and more often they don't. What I often discover is that I'm not always faithful in caring for my part of the process. Instead I blame their poor growth on anything else. Since we now live in the country, I am trying to be more faithful to the caring of my plants around the house. The important thing is, plants need a combination of sunlight, water, feed, fertilizer, pruning, and tender loving care.

It is the same thing in the church. It is easy to get caught up in different leadership personalities in the church. Sometimes we think our church would grow better if we still had the last pastor or two pastors ago. Sometimes we think the music would be better if our director had more, or sometimes less, experience or education. Sometimes we think that only Mrs. Jones knows how to work with the youth, and on and on.

In reality, the Church is the Lord's and we are all instruments working together to serve the Lord to the best of our abilities, however diverse they may be. It is only in working together that the ministry of the church can really happen.

G.M.D.

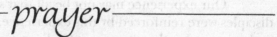

Share together as a prayer Psalm 119:1-8

SING: "Hymn of Promise"

Transforming Moments

2 Peter 1:16-21

Have you ever had a "mountaintop" experience? A time in your life when you felt overwhelmed with the presence of God's Spirit? Some of us have had several such experiences and others of us only one or two, or maybe even none. If you have not had such an experience, I pray that you will, for it brings new insights and understanding to your relationship with God.

Some of my most memorable experiences of the presence of the Holy Spirit came when we were touring the Holy Land, through sharing communion with Palestinian Christians, walking where Jesus had walked, stepping into the empty tomb and knowing that Jesus risen to glory after accepting my sins on the cross. Other times have been in the midst of working with God's people, especially in a retreat type setting or small group gathering. Other times have been when I have been alone out in God's world.

That special presence of the Holy Spirit doesn't come only at times of great joy or high moments, but even at the depth of despair; a time when everything seems totally void or empty and you are not sure in what direction to go. The Lord can touch you in a special way and bring new meaning and confirmation for your life.

For Jesus the experience of God's presence, as well as Moses and Elijah, was a confirmation that the time was now to fulfill all that God had sent him to do. This experience was shared with Peter, James, and John, so that they might also understand all that Jesus was sent to do for God.

Our experience may not be all that spectacular, but just as the disciples were reinforced by this experience, so we can be reinforced and encourage others to accept God's presence always with us.

G.M.D.

A Repentant Heart

Psalm 51:10-13

A couple of months ago there was an episode of *Touched by an Angel* where Monica was sharing in a therapy group how she had been gluttonous and drunk several cups of Cappuccino and was truly sorry for what she had done. Well, only an angel could have so little to feel guilty about.

We often make mistakes in our daily lives by saying or doing something that hurts someone else. Sometimes an apology may take care of the problem, but, sometimes that might not be enough. We may carry a heavy feeling of guilt or hurt and don't know how to let it go. Ash Wednesday is a perfect time for us to look at ourselves and honestly lay before the Lord the mistakes we have made or the grudges we are carrying.

A friend was sharing with us how she had taught her children that when we ask forgiveness for a wrong, it is like it never happened. The child had been scolded and then asked forgiveness from her mother about a mistake she had made. When her father came home, and the mother was sharing what the daughter had done, the father went to the child and asked what she had done. Her response was, "What mistake? It's been washed away." That is the kind of forgiveness God will give us when we ask him.

As a special group of caring friends, you may want to take time to write down anything you want to change or get rid of in your life and place the paper in a bowl or basket and together ask the Lord to forgive your mistakes and renew your hearts that you may humbly prepare yourselves for this Lenten season.

G.M.D.

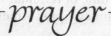

Sing together in an attitude of prayer "Breathe on Me, Breath of God"

Watch Out for the Tempter

Matthew 4:1-11

A friend, Jim, who had two children and a lovely wife, had been working for the same company as a sales representative for several years and was comfortably successful financially. His boss called him in and praised the work he had been doing, and offered him a much larger district with greater responsibilities, a substantial increase in salary, and bonus possibilities. Jim was already working more hours than his family liked. This new position would require even more time away from home. His boss tried to convince him it was the best thing for his family. Jim and his wife talked it over and decided he would not take the new position. His boss could not understand how he would turn down such a good opportunity. It is very difficult in our materialistic world to resist the temptation to want more and more no matter what the cost.

One of the greatest temptations we face in the church is to try to provide everything for everybody with the best possible facility. We don't want the neighboring churches to outdo us. Even within our choirs we sometimes want to be the best choir in our area. We pride ourselves that we do "better" music than our neighboring church choirs and even the church across town. When we become more concerned about how well we sound than singing praises to the Lord, we have yielded to the tempter. We want always to do our best for the Lord, but we need to watch out that we aren't tempted to do our best for our own glory rather than the Lord's glory.

G.M.D.

---

prayer

Lord, as we begin this season of Lent, help us to always keep our hearts in line with you. Help us to seek always to sing to your honor and glory and to trust that your Holy Spirit will fill those who listen. Thank you for this time of renewal. We are your servants in Jesus Christ's name, in whom we pray. Amen.

SING: "When I Survey the Wondrous Cross"

Just Plain Faith

Psalm 121 and John 3:16-17

Recently my husband, Doc, and I retired from our positions in the church and moved to our present home in northeast Georgia, right in the middle of the mountains. When I first looked at our log home, it was the mountains that captured my heart and Psalm 121 quickly came to mind. We have made our home into a small bed and breakfast and everyone who visits us has a similar feeling of God's presence surrounding this place. It has been much more difficult to provide a living income than we had anticipated. There was a great deal of repair work to do, as well as reconstruction we need for the bed and breakfast. Even though there are times we are not sure that we will be able to stay, we know that as long as our faith remains in the Lord, his will for our lives will be worked out. Knowing the Lord Jesus Christ in our hearts and souls and trusting fully in God's constant care, we greet each new day with joy and love in our hearts, ready to serve however God asks. God has given us many wonderful opportunities to serve wherever we are.

When you can fully commit your life to Christ in all areas of your life, you can understand the peace and joy that this commitment will bring. For God so loved the world (us) that he gave his only Son (Jesus Christ) that whoever (you and me) believes in him will not perish but have everlasting (including a full and joyful life now). THANKS BE TO GOD!!!

G.M.D.

prayer

Gracious God, help us always to trust in your love and guiding hand in all we do. Sometimes we try to take the control for our lives from you and do things our way. Help us, Lord, to know that you are always there to guide us in all areas of our lives. Help us also to be the servants you would have us to be. As a part of your church, we seek only to do your will in sharing your Word with your people. Be with us now in Jesus', our Lord and Savior's name. Amen.

SING: "Great Is Thy Faithfulness"

Faith Brings Joy

Romans 5:1-5

We enjoy the peace that comes from being made right with God, but we still face daily problems that help us grow. As we come close to Passion week, we have mixed feelings, both the sorrow that Jesus is about to face but also we know the joy that comes at the resurrection.

Our joy depends on our knowing Jesus Christ and because of this knowledge we can face most anything. Even as we try to serve the Lord in the church we sometimes face more hurdles to climb before we finally accomplish our project or program.

This past Christmas Doc and I were trying to put together the Journey to Bethlehem for our church. First, as is often true, we could only get three to commit to help. After much begging from different classes we got the commitment we needed. Then we found there had been some mix-up in scheduling, and we couldn't get the hall to set up and do a run-through until the afternoon of the presentation. It was only through the presence of the Holy Spirit that the journey went as well as it did. It was only the presence of the Holy Spirit in our lives that we knew we could make it through.

So often we face personal or group situations that seem impossible to work through, but the Lord always shows us a way to overcome. Each time we struggle through a problem, we can reflect on how the knowledge of the presence of the Lord in our lives has helped us to gain strength and grow in our faith and understanding of others. The assurance of Christ in our lives gives us continued hope in all things.

G.M.D.

prayer

Gracious and Loving God, we rejoice at your constant presence in our lives. Whatever problems we face, you are always there to help us through, whether they are little or great, you give us the strength and understanding to overcome. Lord, we pray that we may be worthy to serve you always. Amen.

SING: "My Hope Is Built"

What is Blindness?

John 9:1-7

One of the monologues I enjoy doing is Fanny Crosby, the blind poet and song writer. Fanny's eyes were scarred by a wrong application of a poltice by her doctor, when she was only a few months old. That left her almost completely blind. Her love of the Lord and her desire to be a writer helped her to overcome her handicap and become one of the best known hymn writers ever. Her greatest revelation came when she realized that her love of the Lord and her life in the world are one. Then all her writing took on new meaning and was written only for the glory of the Lord. Fanny may have been blind in her eyes, but her heart could see the real light, the light of Christ.

Sometimes we become blinded by the world around us and it becomes difficult for us to see where we are going. If we can keep the light of Christ burning strongly in our hearts, he will never fail to show us the way.

One of the problems choirs face everywhere, is getting stuck in the "music-rut." We tend to do the same music over and over because we think we can do it better than something new. If we get stuck with our music, our vision becomes blurred in our faith as well. It is important for us to always be open to the Holy Spirit's leading, in our faith and in our music.

G.M.D.

prayer

Loving and all-knowing God, you have given us eyes to see with, ears to hear with, voices to sing your praises with, and a heart to know you with. Help us always to understand that it is in the knowing you that makes all things around us beautiful. Fill us with your grace as we seek to serve you always.

SING: "To God be the Glory"

Life is Worth Living Well

Romans 8:6-11

I have a friend who is very attractive, has a beautiful voice, is highly intelligent, but is burdened by problems in her personal life. Her husband abandoned the family but still makes unreal demands of her regarding their children. The financial and emotional demands of this situation have completely stifled her growth in the rest of her life. There is no question that she is in a very hard situation. She has always had a strong faith and she continues to attend church on a regular basis. Somehow, though, she is not able to allow the Lord to help her carry her burden and return to being the beautiful, capable women he made her to be. My heart aches for her and I pray that she will open her heart to the living presence of the Holy Spirit once more.

Her story is not uncommon. Many people are so weighed down with the trials and pressures of this life that they find it very difficult to get out from under their stifling burdens of care. If you find yourself in that situation, remember that the only way any of us can regain the fullness of life is through the power and presence of the Holy Spirit.

As we seek to know more fully all that the resurrected Christ means in our lives, may we in turn pray for and offer help to those around us who are struggling with the burdens of this life. Every time we stand to lead in worship, let us do so in an attitude of prayer, asking God to use us to lighten the load others carry.

G.M.D.

SING: "What Wondrous Love Is This"

The Parade Begins

Matthew 21:1-11

Have you ever been caught in the middle of a village parade as you were trying to drive through the town. Most of the time we become annoyed at the delay, but sometimes if it is an exciting parade we may get out of the car and enjoy watching. We may not know the significance of many of the floats or groups that pass, but it is fun to watch. When we continue on our way we may have come away with a totally different idea of what the parade was all about than the real meaning of the parade for the local people.

When Jesus entered Jerusalem on that day, riding on the back of a colt, many watchers missed the whole meaning of the "parade." Still today, many people do not understand all that was happening. It is important to recognize that the donkey was a symbol of an animal of peace, whereas the horse was an animal of war. Jesus was stating that he was coming in peace. Jesus knew that this was likely to be his last time to come to Jerusalem and that this was the beginning of the end of his earthly ministry. The calls of the people were for him to save them as much as shouts of joy. Hosanna actually means "save us." What more appropriate call to shout to the Savior, than "save us." What they didn't understand, is that his saving power would come through his death and resurrection and not from an earthly war on evil oppression.

When we sing "Hosanna, Loud Hosanna" this week, we must sing it with a sense of the saving power of the Lord Jesus Christ.

G.M.D.

prayer

Precious Lord, give us an understanding of all you have done for us through your son, Jesus Christ. We often get so caught up in the celebration of the day, that we overlook all that the day really means in your saving grace. Thank you, God, for loving us and giving us your son, Jesus Christ, in whose name we pray. Amen.

The Ultimate Plot

John 19:1-11

Remember when you were a teenager and you wanted to be sure you got to do what you wanted, even though you knew your mother did not want you to do it? You would find a way to use your friends and even your father, if you were clever enough, to somehow get your mother to agree to your request. We are very good at figuring out plots to get our own way. They don't always work, but sometimes we get lucky, or so we think. More often than not, what we manage to plot out will cause us a bigger problem than if we had not done it.

The religious leaders made sure they had covered both the Jewish and the Roman side of the desire to have Jesus crucified. Accusing Jesus of blasphemy satisfied the Jews as a reason to crucify him and accusing Jesus of causing rebellion satisfied the Romans as a reason to have him crucified. They thought that they had won either way. What they did not realize was that God was the one who was really in power. It was God who turned their plot to kill Jesus into the resurrection and victory over death and sin. God is always ultimately in charge and can always use our bad judgment for good.

As we meditate on all that this day represents, may we be mindful of how we are sometimes too quick to judge someone else's actions without really understanding the whys of those actions. As leaders within the church, we need to be examples to those who are growing in their faith. We should always try to see all sides of a situation.

G.M.D.

---

prayer

Great God, we come on bended knee, humbly before you. Help us to always seek your guidance in all we do. It is hard for us to grasp all that you have done for us and especially the willingness to go to the cross for us. May we strive to do our best for you in all things in grateful thanks and praise to you, God Almighty, Father, Son and Holy Spirit. Amen.

SING: "To Mock Your Reign, O Dearest Lord"

Victory for Our God

Acts 10:34-43

For a time I was privileged to serve as choral director in a small Lutheran church shortly after the publication of their latest hymnal. One of the favored formats for Holy Communion includes the hymn "This Is the Feast of Victory." The music is very uplifting and the text by John W. Arthur adapted from Revelations contains what might well have been Peter's title for his brief sermon to Cornelius and his household: "This is the feast of victory for our God. Alleluia!" Peter proclaims that we who have witnessed the life, death and resurrection of Jesus Christ must now testify, and one of Arthur's verses enjoins us to "Sing with all the people of God." A church choir could hardly expect a clearer mandate!

Sometimes all the attendance expectations for special services don't seem like such a blessing. Let's consider the possibility that your choir may have been involved in as many as four or five special services during Holy Week, including Maundy Thursday and Good Friday. If you have been privileged, as Peter and the other disciples were, to witness these things, is it possible that God has chosen you to testify even as God chose them? How much more joyful and fulfilled are our Easter "Alleluias" when we have felt in our music the despair of Good Friday! From such a perspective, our service in the choir is indeed a blessing and privilege.

Someone has defined "Hallelujah" as "Yea, God!" The Easter celebration has long been the central event in Christianity. Let's not forget who did it, nor that this active God has also commanded us to testify. The entire Easter season must be one of joyful testimony, and Easter Sunday is only the beginning.

H.W.D.

prayer

Almighty God, you came first to the Hebrew people, but now we may all know your presence when we seek you. Thank you for the ability and opportunities to praise you and your resurrected Son in our singing. May our "Alleluia" lift others in heart and soul, to truly give you all the glory and praise due your name. Amen.

SING: "This Is the Feast of Victory"

When Faith Becomes Sight

1 Peter 1:3-9

The Second Sunday of Easter is known as "Faith Sunday" and each year in the lectionary one of the lessons is John's account of Jesus' first appearance to the disciples which Thomas missed. The response of Thomas to the report of a resurrected Jesus has earned him the unfortunate title of "Doubting Thomas." Thus, from year to year we hear sermons on the negative nature of doubt, the positive results of healthy doubt, and the importance of believing without physically seeing. This lesson from Jesus is clearly reflected in Peter's letter.

Peter speaks of the trials of life as a Christian which we all must face to a lesser or greater degree. Our faith and rejoicing must fill our entire life, for salvation to eternal life is ours even through trials and temptations, thanks to the resurrection of Jesus. As a title of a book proclaims, *Hallelujah Anyhow!*

Although this is the Easter Season, the idea of believing without seeing recalls for me the delightful Christmas-time film, "The Santa Clause." On one level the story reflects a man's journey from doubt, fear of personal loss and of rejection, to a new life of great fulfillment and joy shared with others. To accomplish this, however, he must come to realize fully Christ's admonition as proclaimed by the elf, Judy. She tells Scott Calvin that, as a typical skeptical adult, he has missed the point: "Seeing is not believing. Believing is seeing." Granted he receives plenty of physical evidence of his transformation from Scott Calvin to Santa Claus. Nevertheless, well before the eleven-month preparation period has lapsed, Scott seems at peace with any trials of rejection or separation and is ready to share the new life he now believes he is destined to live. At the risk of trivializing Jesus' and Peter's message by this comparison, we too must make our peace with the world of trial and temptation. We are destined to rejoice in the life of salvation made evident to us in the Easter story.

H.W.D.

prayer

Dear Lord, you ask us to believe that which we cannot see. But we can have newly opened eyes if we accept your Easter salvation, and believing becomes our way of life. Help us to know your forgiveness, support, and presence even in times of trial and doubt. Transform our life into one that truly reflects the joy of your salvation. Help us share that joy in all our work for you. Amen.

SING: "Come Ye Faithful, Raise the Strain"

When Charity Does Begin at Home

Psalm 116

Let's face it: Being in the church choir puts us in a vulnerable position and in a position of sometimes overwhelming responsibility. We are vulnerable to the likes and desires of the pastor and the congregation, not to mention what the director expects. We are vulnerable especially to the messages from the pulpit because it seems we are always present. The preacher's messages sometimes seem to target us or might trigger a defensive attitude prompted by some personal sensitivity, maybe even feelings of guilt. The congregation's response or lack thereof to our music could trigger feelings of despair or even resentment at being unappreciated for our efforts and dedication. After all, we think, our Easter music was great but we still don't have any new choir members. And so, we can sympathize with the psalmist: "All humans are a vain hope."

But then there are times when we can truly ride the waves of blessing from God and God's people. Our witness before our sisters and brothers in the church is indeed important, to them, to us, and thus, to God. Surely, we must testify outside the church family, but all the New Testament lessons for this week make note of congregational life and its importance is implied. The psalmist even repeats in verses 14 and 18 his determination to fulfill vows in the presence of all God's people. Surely he meant to have us hear that vow, and we can take it as a challenge to do likewise.

In this Easter season we too must recognize the deliverance from eternal death noted by the psalmist. He was both testifying and prophesying. Thanks to Christ's resurrection, we now know the fulfillment of the prophecy. It is our responsibility to testify to it "in the courts of the house of the Lord." And when the Easter even becomes a reality in our lives, this responsibility can become our desire as well.

H.W.D.

prayer

Dear Lord, we have witnessed your resurrection. We pray that we may know anew your resurrection within us. We recognize the responsibility we have to testify to your salvation. Forgive us when we see it as only a responsibility. Help us make it our vow and better still our desire. Accept the service we bring for the uplifting of your Holy Name among your blessed people. Amen.

SING: "Easter People, Raise Your Voices"

Abundant Life

Acts 2:42-47

To experience and then to express abundant life is among the great privileges of Christian discipleship. In this week's lessons, John tells how the Good Shepherd is our guide, while Peter's letter emphasizes that Christ, our example, in suffering, gives us healing, becoming our soul's shepherd and guardian for abundant life. In the Acts scripture we can see how the abundant life was enacted by the infant church, primarily in unity and sharing of resources of all sorts. It is clear that from the beginning, unity and caring have been the keys to an abundant life in all aspects of Christian living.

As a choir member and director, I have become well aware of how wonderful are our opportunities for unity and caring. In both small and very large groups, relationships between members influence one's sense of well-being and effectiveness. Performance of music by its very nature requires a unified expression, giving the musician experiences in this area that may be envied by non-performers. Beyond this is the sense of belonging and making a valued contribution to the group's efforts. In our experience, a very large symphonic chorus made us aware how valuable this sense can be. Consequently, in forming our own community chorus to perform major choral works, one of the goals was to promote genuine personal relationships and mutual respect and support. Not only was performance musically rewarding, but even after we had to move away the group maintains a life of its own with a new director.

Within the church we are compelled by Christ's example and leadership to seek and promote mutual caring and unity. The result is but one small example of abundant life.

H.W.D.

---

prayer

Lead us, O Good Shepherd, that we may find the pastures you have prepared for us. Help us to share what we find there with others that our testimony through our music may truly reflect your loving care. Amen.

SING: "When in Our Music God Is Glorified"

Living Stones or Slippery Gravel?

1 Peter 2:2-10

Look around your choir and you will likely see members who hold very important positions on various boards and committees of your church. The people in the choir are usually among the most active and respected persons in a local church, and many may even represent their church on broader church and community organizations. Members of the choir, whether or not they hold other posts, are the living stones of which Peter speaks. The very fact that the choir seeks to enhance other believers' worship experiences makes each one an important building block.

Of course, we could become a stumbling block if we are not careful. We are cautioned always to proclaim God's glory, to be more than just another great singing group. Further, our example in attendance at practices and worship serves as a challenge to other believers. Our example in caring and unity for others in the choir and persons in the church will contribute to the total church as well.

At our present home, we have a rather steep drive up from the road to the house and barn. When you enter and climb the drive you note that the rather large gravel stones, although they look nice, tend to make traction a little unsure. If you try to go too fast, you may slip and spin, and if you go too slowly, you may not make the climb at all. So too in our Christian living, we must be careful not to charge ahead too fast, nor should we drag along too slowly. Doing either of these we could become like the gravel in our driveway causing others to slip and spin out of control. We must aid them to make their life's climb at a steady, moderated speed toward the goal of God's eternal glory.

Our secure placement as living stones in the church rather than slippery gravel of life's climb will make a great contribution to the growth of faith within our church.

H.W.D.

---

prayer

Dear Lord, we pray for all those who hold positions of leadership in your church. May we all know the security of your Son as our cornerstone against whom we may rest and by whom we can line up and guide our life. Help us to lend our secure placement in faith to others, and not to be slippery gravel as they travel life's upward path. We give all glory to you and your resurrected Son. Amen.

SING: "Christ Is Made the Sure Foundation"

Every Time I Feel the Spirit

John 14:15-21

Have you ever wondered how it is that the deepest response you may have personally to music is to some quiet choral piece, whereas the congregation compliments you more profusely on some highly rhythmic or full-voiced piece that moved you somewhat less? Welcome to the varied movements of God's Spirit in your music. The temptation is then to do the more dramatic rather than the quieter choral piece, given the choice of music for some Sunday service. But our music must always seek to reflect the varied levels of receptiveness among all the worshipers ourselves included. We probably cannot accomplish this all in one service, but over the weeks of our presentations in worship we should be able to reach out with a variety to the varied souls we serve.

How do we find the spirit for all our music, whatever the style? John's gospel may just have the prescription for finding the spirit, whether in our music or in our lives. The beginning and end of our effort must be love, love for Christ Jesus, for the Father, and for one another. Every piece of music must be prepared, not only for the best performance of notes and style, but also with love for what it attempts to say in a worship setting. It behooves us all, then, to seek out music truly worthy of our loving preparation and presentation as worship, whatever its style.

In addition, we see from John that we must keep Jesus' commandments and we must accept the Spirit as a gift in answer to his prayer. The love we show for one another, the unity and caring we share within our choir and throughout the church, and the service we do in mission and outreach efforts of our church are in response to Jesus' commandments. Accepting the Spirit as a gift must not stop at Jesus' prayer, however. We must continually pray, as he promises to do on our behalf, that what we do may be Spirit-led and Spirit-filled.

Only when we operate in love, keeping Jesus' commandments and receiving the Spirit as a gift, will both our personal lives and choral life in worship become evidence to ourselves and others of God's Holy Spirit in our presence. H.W.D.

prayer

SING: "Spirit of God, Descend Upon My Heart"

An Upper Room for the Choir?

Acts 1:6-14

How often do we take some member of the family or a good friend to the airport and just drop them at the terminal door? In our family it is the custom to accompany the traveler all the way to the boarding gate, getting in as much conversation as possible before the final parting. We know what is about to happen, but not so the disciples in our scripture. It may have seemed they were on their way to Bethany, home of Lazarus and his sisters. They may have stopped momentarily for Jesus to instruct them, seemingly much as in the past. And off he goes! Is it any wonder that it took a couple of angels to get their attention back to earth? And it is no wonder that they felt the urgency to return to their upper room for prayer and to begin some planning for their new tasks. They are now on their own—or so it seems.

We can take seriously Jesus' promise to send the power of the Holy Spirit, but at the time it was a promise, and the disciples had just been warned not to look for some spectacular take-over of a restored Israel. So prayer and preparation were all they could do! These are also the means by which our testimony will be empowered.

We all know that our rehearsals and other practices are important for preparing for our witness in worship. We personally and collectively can take a lesson from the other aspect of the disciple's gatherings. Prayer continues to be an essential ingredient to open our hearts to the coming of the Spirit and thereby empower us to effectively lead the music of worship. In a sense, our choral time can be our time in the "upper room" preparing for witness. Seen in this way, the fellowship, rehearsal, and sharing can lead us to continual renewal and growing effectiveness in our worship leadership. Every aspect of our gathering, warm-up music practice, and prayer will then enrich and empower our testimony.

H.W.D.

prayer

Dear Lord, we come together looking to improve our service for you in your church. Bring our minds and hearts back to earth where we are commanded to witness to your people. Help us to share our mutual joys and concerns and to prepare our whole selves for the coming of your Holy Spirit. In that coming, we may be empowered anew to be faithful witnesses for you in our service of worship. All this we pray in the name of our resurrected and ascended Lord. Amen.

SING: "Spirit of the Living God"

Talented or Gifted?

1 Corinthians 12:3*b*-13

Have you ever looked around at the faces in a performing group? It seems that there are a lot of relatively bored people making some absolutely gorgeous music. Then there are those who are clearly engrossed in and captivated by the music they are producing or witnessing. I don't believe I have ever watched a top-level performer, a virtuoso, who looked bored by their own or the surrounding performers' efforts. The talent of the bored or non-engrossed performer might not be a question, but that person's spirit for the music certainly may be.

Our presentations in worship cannot ever be without spirit and certainly will require *the* Spirit to be effective. Pentecost Sunday is the day we are reminded of the power of the Holy Spirit to affect people. In our reading of the original Pentecost story, Paul points out that God is the one and only source and the Holy Spirit is the same, whatever the gift expressed may be. We are fortunate to be able to focus a talent through a spiritual gift, that of service in our worship leadership.

The truly astounding aspect of the Spirit's coming is that we have done nothing to earn that Spirit. Granted we have prepared ourselves in rehearsal and at prayer. It is, even as at the Easter miracle, God's doing. We have opened our hearts and minds in prayer and made ready the basic vehicle for our testimony in worship, just as did the disciples. Now the gift of the Spirit can move in and through us to make our little talent so much more as we form one body, the choir, in service and testimony to our sisters and brothers in the congregation.

H.W.D.

prayer

Heavenly Father, we pray that your Holy Spirit may find us ready to accept the gifts you give us. In this day when we commemorate the outpouring of Your Spirit on the disciples and the birth of your New Testament church, help us feel a new birth as well. May we be ever grateful for your gifts to us and may our talents be empowered by your Spirit in a way that expresses your love to all who hear us. In Jesus' holy name we pray. Amen.

SING: "Every Time I Feel the Spirit"

How Do We Say Good-bye?

Matthew 28:16-20

Class is over and before the students leave the room the teacher gives them an assignment to complete before next they meet. Mom or Dad leaves the house and gives the kids a task to do while they remain at home, or the kids leave the house and Mom tells them to be careful. Radio and television personalities often close their programs with some kind of admonition. In Jesus' final words, Matthew reports Jesus' claim to all authority and his orders to make disciples, baptizing and teaching all nations. In addition to the unique claim to universal authority or power, Jesus asserts that he will be with us at all times. No one else can make such a claim.

Based on these claims, we can have the assurance that our efforts will not go unrewarded. We can work together at whatever the task or activity set for us in our service as a choir and know that, with the balance of prayer and preparation, we most certainly can succeed: we can move people spiritually by our music.

Based on these claims, we must know equally well what the purpose of our efforts should be, to what end we prepare and present our service. We work "in the name of the Father and of the Son and of the Holy Spirit." What an intimidating task! But now we know this, we know how our work must be done for we are no longer the center of our own efforts. Our singing must be in and for the worship of God. Consequently, everything we do must be prepared well and with sincerity to touch others spiritually.

Have you ever had the experience of working hard on the upcoming anthem and other service music but when you come to the benediction response you seem to just settle for something familiar or easy? On occasion, we have probably all been guilty of that. Or we come to the end of the service and think more about what happens after church than what we are singing, often because we are almost too familiar with it to feel a need for concentration. If all our music is service to God, our final words will certainly be a benediction, a "good saying," and our "Amen" will surely be the affirmation of God's will it is intended to be.

H.W.D.

prayer

Gracious God, we pray that we may accept the challenge to do all to your greater glory. Help us never to be lackadaisical about our service for we do it for you. Make us attentive to your call and to our Lord's great commission, and help us to begin that service within our own church. Amen.

SING: "Lord, You Give the Great Commission"

Actions Speak Louder Than Words

Matthew 7:21-29

I remember a movie a long time ago when Dean Martin and Jerry Lewis were a comedy team. Jerry's character was playing in a football game and, of course, when he got the ball, he ran the full length of the field in the wrong direction, making a goal for the other team. He obviously didn't understand the rules of the game very well. In any sport you have to understand exactly what is expected of each player and how that fits with the whole team.

Being in a choir is something like being a member of a sports team, in that there are certain things you must do to be part of the whole "team." Imagine what would happen to a choir if everyone decided to do things just as they wanted. Suppose, for instance, one person, who perhaps had a degree in music, decided to sing the piece in a different tempo from everyone else. Or suppose a section, say the alto section, decided to sing the notes written from another section. Utter chaos! I'm sure the director would deny knowing any of them!

Jesus was talking about just such people, those who professed to be doing work in his name but did not understand who he was and what he was all about. Jesus asks us for our obedience in serving him, putting our lives in his hands, believing in who he is, and living our lives in response to that faith.

When a choir follows the direction of their director and trusts in the director's judgment, the music produced will be harmonious music. When we follow and trust the direction of Christ in our lives, then we will have harmony in our daily living as Christ would have us.

H.W.D.

prayer

Loving God, help us always to be willing to listen to your voice in all we do. We pray that we do not seek to always try to show others that we are always right, but are willing to listen to those who seek to guide us in your will. Thank you for giving us continued opportunities to fulfill our commitment to you. Be with us now, in Jesus' name. Amen.

SING: "Trust and Obey"

All Are Welcome

Matthew 9:9-13

My first position as a D.C.E. in the church was in a town in upstate New York. I was in charge of was the youth program. We had decided we were going to do a drama for the church. At the same time I had been asked to visit a former member of the church, a young man recovering from back surgery. I discovered that he loved drama and invited him to come and share with the rest of the youth in presenting our production. When I told the youth that he wanted to share with us, a resounding NO went out. This boy had been involved with the Satanic church and they wanted nothing to do with him. I convinced them that this might be a way to bring him back to Christ. He shared in the production and we did open the door back to Christ. The pastor of the church was not at all pleased with what I had done. He was also upset because some young people I was trying to help had some alcohol and drug problems. When he showed his strong concern for my inappropriate behavior, I asked him if we were not in the church to help those who had gone astray? His response was that it looked bad for the church. Needless to say, I didn't stay at that church very long. I know Jesus has called us to help any who have strayed or who don't know Christ.

When we make a commitment to serve Christ in any way, whether it is as a D.C.E., a pastor, a choir director, or a choir member, we are making the same commitment to share in whatever way we can to help others know the Lord Jesus Christ. One of the ways we can do that in the choir is to reach out to those who are not a part of any church and encourage them to come and share with us as a part of Christ's family. There are so many outside our church who are afraid to become a part of our church or a part of our choir because they don't think they are good enough. The choir is a wonderful way to help others know the joy and fellowship of being a part of Christ's family. Don't be afraid to let the Holy Spirit lead you to others for Christ.

I have been personally blessed with sharing Christ with so many people. Some have gone into full time ministry, some have taken responsibilities in their churches as teachers, choir members, youth workers and on and on. When the Holy Spirit enters a new life, anything is possible. Never underestimate the power of the Holy Spirit!   G.M.D.

---

prayer

Lord, fill us with your Holy Spirit that we may always be open to those around us who do not know you or who are lost in their journey of life. Help us always to know it is you we serve. Help us not to overlook those around us who need your love as we are able to share. May we ever grow more and more in your love through your Holy Spirit. Amen.

SING: "A Charge to Keep I Have"

Surely You Don't Mean Me?

Matthew 9:35–10:1

I went to the Course of Study at Emory University in Atlanta, Georgia several years back. I already had a Masters Degree in Christian education and had taken several courses at Vanderbilt University in Nashville, Tennessee. I felt pretty good about my educational accomplishments. My first class threw me a real curve. At least half of my class at Emory had only a high school education and were already serving in a church as a pastor. I could not understand how these poorly educated people could have been called by God to serve in a church without having completed some kind of advanced education. As the summer went on, I had a very important insight. As my classmates shared about their different churches and the work they were doing, I saw how God uses all kinds of people, with all different backgrounds and education, to reach others. It was a very enlightening experience for me. Jesus began, right from the beginning, to call unlikely people to go out and reach others for him. He continues to call all kinds of people to serve him. The important thing is, are we ready to respond when he calls us?

One of the most common responses you hear in any church when one is asked to serve in some specific way is, "I'm not qualified to do that, why don't you ask Sally? She could be so much better at that job." My good friend and Sunday school superintendent of one of the churches I was privileged to serve, put her finger on the best response. She said, "God doesn't call the qualified, he qualifies the one he calls." How true that is! God will never ask us to do anything without giving us the means to do it. It is important to always seek to do more than we think we are capable of. The choir is a wonderful place to stretch your abilities beyond what you've always done. Maybe you can find a way to go beyond the church to share your music of praise with others, like going to nursing homes or shut-ins. Let the Lord lead you in new ways to reach out.   G.M.D.

prayer

Lord help us to reach beyond our comfortable zone. So often we like to do only what we are familiar with and never seek to do anything extra for you. Lord, we are ready to hear your voice and do what you would have us do to share your Word to those who are unable to get out or to those who have never heard. We are your servants Lord, and want to serve you in whatever way you call us. In Jesus' name we pray. Amen.

SING: "Where He Leads Me"

It's Not Always Easy

Matthew 10:24-39

One of my dear friends at Scarritt College in the mid seventies, was Maggie Muzorewa. Her husband is Bishop Muzorewa, who was then also interim Prime Minister of Rhodesia as it became Zimbabwe. The bishop was first a Christian and then a politician. This strong commitment to Christ got him arrested more than once. He spent time in solitary confinement because of his faith. He never faltered in his faith in all this time. When we got to know him personally, he shared with us how he would recite Scripture to himself and pray in order to keep his sanity until his release. He knew that following Christ would not be easy in a country that did not yet know Christ well. He also reminded us that Jesus told us that we would have to suffer if we were willing to be his followers. All of the disciples ended up being martyred for their faith, and many Christian leaders since then have continued to be willing to suffer for their faith in Christ that others might know him.

Fortunately we live in a society where there is very little need for the kind of suffering for our faith that others have endured. But, we must be ready as Christians to stand firm for our faith in Christ, even if it may mean rejection by family or friends. It is easier to agree with those we love, even if we know in our hearts they are wrong. Maybe we don't outwardly agree, but we remain silent which is the same as agreement. There are so many wrongs going on around us all the time and if it's hard to stand firm against them by yourself, then turn to each other for support and encouragement to speak for the Lord against the evils of society. Rejoice with your Christian friends that you know and love the Lord Jesus Christ.

G.M.D.

prayer

Gracious and Loving God, we pray for your strength to always be ready to stand firm for you. There are so many who do not know your love and the joy that comes from knowing you. Help us to always be ready to serve you and share your love in a way that others can see your love in us. We pray always in your Son, Jesus Christ's name. Amen.

SING: "Are Ye Able"

The Reward of Service

Matthew 10:40-42

When my girls were in middle school, I headed up a 4-H club in our community. At Christmas time we decided to go caroling in the village. One of the houses we stopped at was just up the road from where we lived. It was a big old house where an older lady lived, who everyone saw as unfriendly. We started to sing at her house and there was no acknowledgement of our presence until we were about to leave. The woman came out and said her mother wanted us to come in. We didn't even know she had a mother living. We were a little scared when we went in, not knowing what to expect. Her mother was very elderly and began to cry because she hadn't had anyone sing carols to her in such a long time. We sang several carols for them and then Loraine showed us around her house. As we were about to leave, Loraine began to cry and shared with me that she had broken her shoulder and wasn't able to make anything for her mother for Christmas. I asked if we could come back on Christmas morning to bring some cookies for her mother. The girls were all excited about what they could make or do for these two ladies for Christmas. We made cookies and candy and decorated a small Christmas tree. Then we made a gift for Loraine and her mother and I wrapped a hand knit sweater for Loraine to give to her mother. When we went back on Christmas morning with all our gifts, Loraine could hardly speak. Her joy was no greater than our joy when we saw what it meant to the two of them. That is the kind of reward we always get when we do something meaningful for someone else with no expectation of any kind of return.

One of the greatest rewards we receive in the choir is when we have done a really fine performance of some piece of music and know in our hearts that it was good. The reward is doubled when the congregation shares with us how meaningful the music was or how well the choir sounded this morning. We don't sing to be rewarded, as singing the Lord's praise is a reward in itself, but it is always nice to know that others found our message meaningful. God gives us many rewards along the way as we serve. Many times these rewards come very unexpectedly and we are blessed.

G.M.D.

prayer

Loving Lord, you have blessed us in so many ways. We are able to share our faith freely and have opportunity to sing your praises with others who know and love you. Help us to rejoice in all the many blessings that we receive day by day. Be with us as we share your praise in Jesus' name. Amen.

SING: "Come We That Love the Lord"

Throw Off Your Heavy Yoke

Matthew 11:25-30

As I write this devotion today, our country is celebrating two very important occasions. The installation of President Clinton for his second term, and the recognition of Martin Luther King day. These are wonderful symbols of what it means to throw off your heavy burdens of inappropriate oppressions and ideas that do not fit into the meaning and understanding of a truly Christian nation. How blessed we are to be a free nation. At the same time it is so hard for many to let go of old feelings of resentment and separation. It is not only in our nation or in groups of individual people that we experience these inappropriate burdens on others but within our churches and church groups.

Jesus tells us we must not be blinded by our own knowledge and self importance, for we can miss the true meaning of all that Jesus was trying to share with us. When we think we have all the answers, we are closed to hearing anything new. It is important to always be open to new insights as to how we can further God's kingdom here on earth. Jesus is calling for us to let go of any old laws or ideas that will keep us from truly understanding the full joy of Christ's love. Jesus tells us that when we take on his yoke or mantel, we will know rest for our souls. What greater peace is there than to have the peace in our souls from this gentle and humble Christ?

G.M.D.

prayer

Gracious God, help us to see beyond our own self-centered ideas and ways of doing, that we might more fully understand all that you have promised to us through your Son. We pray that we may always serve you as you would have us serve. Help us to be open to new insights and understandings of your work and love. We pray always in your Son's name. Amen.

SING: "We Shall Overcome"

Seeds Sold Here

Matthew 13:1-9

There is a neat story from the book *Taking Flight* by Anthony DeMello, about the dream of a woman. She dreams that she is in a seed store to buy some seeds and to her surprise the one who runs this store is none other than God himself. She asked him what he sold there. God answered that he sold anything her heart desired. She couldn't believe that she was talking face to face with God. She told God that she wanted peace of mind, love, happiness, wisdom, freedom from fear for herself and all people on earth. God smiled and said, "I think you've got me wrong, my dear. We don't sell fruit here, just seeds."

Jesus' words are the seeds that he tries over and over to plant. You and I are the soil and unless we are ready to receive those words and strive to understand those words through the Spirit of God within us, and seek to nurture those words through prayer, study and fellowship, we can never produce the crop Jesus is talking about.

What is this crop that Jesus wants us to understand? I think is simply that we learn to love and care for each other unconditionally as he has loved us unconditionally.

We are the soil, the ones who will produce the crop or not. We are the ones who will share the love of Christ with others or not. We are the ones who Jesus has entrusted with his Word. It's up to us if the crop grows or is choked out by the many problems of our daily life. Jesus has given us the seeds, what kind of crop will we be able to grow where we are?

G.M.D.

prayer

Heavenly God, help us to be open to your Word that we may understand what you are trying to say to us. Help us to know how we may share your Word with others that they may know you better. We thank you for continuing to give us opportunity to serve you in word and song. In Jesus' name we pray. Amen.

SING: "He Leadeth Me: O Blessed Thought"

Real or a Good Imitation?

Matthew 13:24-30

There have been times in my life when I made my living by making wedding gowns and formal wear. Sometimes people would want nothing but real silk or the very best fabrics for their gown. The problem was that they would never want to pay the price for the real thing. I would try to get the best substitute fabric for the best price and most of the time they couldn't tell the difference. Many times I discovered that they told their friends that they had real silk or whatever. Then I would have the same problem to work through with the friend when she wanted something made from only the best. There are so many items in our life that are imitations of the "real thing." Jesus could use anything as an example today.

The important message in this story of the wheat and tares is not the example, but the meaning of what Jesus is trying to say to us. Jesus was talking about people, those who truly know and love the Lord, and those who profess to know and love the Lord and how hard it is to know the difference. Jesus wants us to know that it is not our responsibility to decide who is really a true Christian and who just claims to be. It is for God to make the final judgment for all of us.

One of the biggest problems we see in our churches today are those who think they have the right to decide who is and who is not a worthy Christian. Sometimes people spend so much time trying to decide who is a worthy Christian that they forget to look at themselves. Once we start judging others for their worthiness as an acceptable Christian, we have stepped over our rights as a Christian ourselves. Fortunately, Christ has given us the opportunity to seek forgiveness and renewal when we step out of bounds. What we need to be most concerned with as we share with both true and false Christians, is to do our very best to follow the teachings of Christ as we understand them. We never know when we may change the heart of one who has not understood. It is hard to know who is and who is not a true Christian, so you must always stand strong in your faith.

G.M.D.

prayer

Gracious God, we know we fail to always be what you have called us to be. Help us to be strong in our faith and to look to your Word when we are not sure. We are grateful for the many opportunities you continue to give us to be more loving and caring of your people. Be with us this day as we seek to serve in Jesus' name. Amen.

SING: "Help Us Accept Each Other"

Paying the Price

Matthew 13:31-33, 44-52

As this is the beginning of the choir season for many, this reading provides an opportunity to renew an important issue common to many of our devotional writings. The familiar parables of the hidden treasure and the valuable pearl given us an immediate insight into one of the requirements for life in the Kingdom of Heaven which clearly applies to our choirs: commitment to something of great value. The price paid for the field in which a treasure had been hidden is similar to that paid for the beautiful pearl. In both cases, the finder sold everything he owned in order to obtain the treasured item. Fortunately for us as singers and directors, the monetary requirements of membership in our church choir rarely reaches such a price.

We all know, nevertheless, that the price in commitment to be paid for effective participation in our service of worship can be rather considerable at times. This is, in the experience of each of us, the most important thing keeping people out of the choir loft, second only to a perceived or real lack of singing ability. I'm sure we have all experienced a situation where a family member has scheduled something that conflicts with our rehearsal participation. Or, we ourselves find that the "only time" we can accomplish something or attend some event is opposite rehearsal or worship. We all know people in our church who cannot participate because of work requirements for themselves or their spouse, or because of the schedules of their children. Granted, then, there are legitimate situations that even committed people cannot avoid, but each of us must continually be on our guard against temptations to let our commitment slip.

Our personal musical skills may be such that we feel we can afford to miss a practice now and then. We must evaluate, however, the message about commitment this sends to others in the choir. The Kingdom of Heaven requires us to give our best at all times, to serve one another in unity and love, and to be ready to receive its blessings in all situations.   H.W.D.

---
prayer

Dear Lord, you paid a great price for us to achieve the Kingdom of Heaven. Help us to know how small the cost to us actually is. Help us to renew our commitment to serve together with others in bringing a small taste of our Kingdom to your people in our church. Amen.

SING: "Marching to Zion"

46

How a Little Becomes Enough

Matthew 14:13-21

It didn't seem like much, enough only for one lad to eat when what was needed was for a very sizable crowd. Yet it was brought to Jesus and it was just what he needed. He blessed the small offering and dispensed it by the disciples to the crowd. Consequently, those who received it were satisfied and there was a substantial amount left over for the disciples to collect.

It didn't seem like much of a choir, only about eight to ten or so depending on the week, few of whom had what might actually be considered a "good" voice. Yet, they were willing to give themselves to this service and there were a couple of people for each voice part. They worked hard at our weekly practices and were emboldened by prayers at rehearsal and before Sunday worship. It was clearly a caring, concerned, and close group of Christian friends who met to carry out their chosen service for Christ. From week to week, as they sang their anthems and other service music, their efforts were blessed and became a fulfilling blessing to the congregation. Further, the singers and I were blessed as well, and they led the way in joint community services and witnessing opportunities at holidays and special seasons of the year. It seemed that every time they came together to sing, we were all aware of a continuing blessing to others and ourselves. It remains as a very fulfilling chapter in each of our spiritual and musical lives.

We can all recognize ourselves in the miracle of the loaves and fishes. What we bring may not seem like much but, if we truly bring it to Christ, it will be blessed. Our ability to read music may be limited, our voice may not be solo quality, but Christ can bless it and use it. Our service can be fulfilling testimony to both those we serve and, best of all, to ourselves as well. Certainly, with this dedication to Christ, it also becomes fulfilling to our God.   H.W.D.

prayer

Almighty God, through your Son you do so much with so little. Help us to always recognize that our best efforts, however limited we may think them to be, so long as we truly give of our best, will be received by you and your Son. Given to you, our talents and gifts can be used by the Spirit for the spiritual nourishment of your people, and even we can be truly satisfied. Amen.

SING: "O For a Thousand Tongues to Sing"

Riding the Waves

Matthew 14:22-33

There certainly will be times when we, like Peter, follow the commands of Christ and find ourselves in some trouble. When things seem darkest, as for the disciples in the hours before sunrise, we need help and Christ can come to us. When he does, we must be willing to find out who this is and accept the offer of rescue. Sometimes we make our own solo effort to meet with this Master of all things and find ourselves in very deep difficulty. The only recourse is to cry out and turn ourselves in faith over to the Master and receive our rescue. This is a well-known story of faith and its effects on our personal life, but what about the boat?

As a beginning sailor, I early learned that one must become sensitive to what the boat is going through to keep it upright and on the wind. Consider the choir as a boat set on its way, guided by the eager hands of its members. This boat must work against many forces that surround it. Stormy waters and headwinds make progress difficult to achieve. Possibly we don't have enough crew to work together and assure progress as we would like, but it may be simple outside and natural forces that hold the boat back. The lead soprano or bass may be ill, the organist does not quite get the feel of the rhythm, or the music budget seems to be lacking. The crew catches a dim and possibly frightening view of the Master. The boat slows while someone sets off alone to reach Him. It wallows and pitches in the waves as Christ rescues the faltering seeker. Once the Master reaches the boat, the outside forces no longer counter its progress. They are still there, but now the boat rides over them. In fact, it rides on and through those forces making its headway buoyed up by what challenged it before.

We must set our boat to the task Christ has given us. But we can only make spiritual progress if we have Him in the boat with us. Our prayers and faith in his presence will turn our challenges into opportunities so that our choir and church can go on to the goal set for it, moving on the Spirit's wind.

H.W.D.

prayer

Dear Lord, we would be doing our work for you, but sometimes we get discouraged when things don't seem to work out. Come to us out of the storm and help us turn adversity into opportunity. Help us to recognize and know your presence with us to strengthen and guide us for all our tasks. In your blessed name we pray, Amen.

SING: "Lonely the Boat"

Little Dogs Can Show the Way

Matthew 15:21-28

As grandparents we have the occasionally dubious privilege of watching videos favored by our younger grandchildren. The event recounted in our scripture, healing the daughter of the Canaanite woman, brings to mind some of those stories that touch on prejudice and assistance of others in need. Because of the reference to "little dogs" in this scripture, the story, "Balto," comes to mind. However true to the total story the cartoon may be, there is a statue dedicated to the half-wolf, half-dog that lead a team of sled dogs through incredible weather over very difficult terrain to bring life-saving medicine to children in Nome, Alaska. Many aspects of the true story do parallel the account reported here by Matthew.

We don't know why Jesus did not heed the woman's initial calls for help. This isn't the only report of someone needing help not receiving Jesus' immediate attention, so it seems safe to suggest he was testing her.

The miracle in this story may actually be one we can receive and even repeat, for the woman would not give up. Consider the position in which she places herself by coming as a woman to a man, in a culture that frowned on this behavior. She comes to a man of a nation that held the view that she was possibly less than human. Jesus is reported to have softened what was probably a conventional expression in questioning the fairness of giving the children's food to "little dogs." But she had finally made her way to his very feet; and, she accepted the rather uncomplimentary comparison, turning it to one final plea for help.

We too must accept our unworthiness and note that this is the very reason we can come to Christ. Whatever the plea, it may not be answered at first, second, or even third call. If the call is selfless as the woman's pleas were, we must continue to express ourselves, possibly despite other persons' feelings of inconvenience or discomfort with the need. Christ hears our faith when we come directly to Him.

H.W.D.

prayer

Loving Lord, help us ever to find our way to you, despite things or people that might hold us back. Help us know our unworthiness and bring it to you along with our need. Help us to be selfless in our seeking for your grace that our faith may truly be rewarded. Amen.

SING: "There Is a Balm in Gilead"

Who Do You Say That Jesus Is?

Matthew 16:13-20

When I was a little girl, I went to church and Sunday school every Sunday with my whole family—my mom, dad, four sisters and my brother. We learned many Bible verses, and wonderful stories of Old Testament people, as well as stories of Jesus and his disciples. Even though I learned all these things from a very young age, I did not know Jesus as the Christ until I was a young adult. I spent most of my time alone talking to God. I knew in my head that Jesus was God's son, but I had no real understanding of what that really meant. We learned songs about Jesus, we learned that he wanted us to be "fishers of men," we knew he wanted us to love each other and God. It was easy for me to do all those things for loving others comes very easy for me. The only person I didn't like, was me. When I finally was given the insight by the Holy Spirit that Jesus was not just the Son of God, but the Savior of the world, the Messiah, then everything took on a whole new meaning. I understood that I was created by God and a true child of God. I understood what it meant that Jesus had died on the cross for me, to forgive my sins. I understood what it means to love others as Christ loves us. I couldn't understand what any of this meant until the Holy Spirit gave me the insight.

There are many in our churches who are just like I was in their understanding of Jesus. They have not yet come to know him as the Christ. If you have been given the insight by the Holy Spirit to truly know Jesus as the Christ, don't be afraid to help others to open their hearts to the living power of the Holy Spirit. Knowing Christ is so much more than just knowing about Jesus.

Who do you say that Jesus is?   G.M.D.

prayer

Holy God, help us to know your Son as the true Messiah in our hearts. Help us to share your Son with those who do not yet know him. We have come to love you, Lord, and your people because you have given us the true insight to know that you, the creator God, Jesus the Christ, and the Holy Spirit are one. We love you and thank you for all you have done for us, your sinful people. Forgive us and strengthen us. We pray in Jesus' name. Amen.

SING: "The Gift of Love"

The Meaningful Life

Matthew 16:21-28

Poor Peter must have really been confused when Jesus referred to him as Satan, since it was in just the last passage that Jesus said he would build his church on Peter's understanding that Jesus was the Messiah. Jesus went on to tell him that he was looking at this situation with earthly understanding. We have to stay open all the time to really understand what God is trying to say to us through the power of the Holy Spirit. The way of God is seldom the easy answer. Had Jesus not taken up the cross, he could not have fulfilled all he had been sent to do; taking our sins upon himself that we might have life eternal.

A friend was sharing in our Disciple's class that her first husband had lost his life while serving as a missionary in Africa. Someone said to her, "What a total loss." Fortunately, she has had opportunity to see and hear about the continuation of the work her husband had started almost thirty years ago. His life was anything but a loss! All missionaries know when they go into areas of unrest they are offering their ministry to God, even if it means the loss of their earthly life.

Not all of us are called to put our lives on the line for Christ, but we are called to stand up for what we think Christ would have us do in any situation. Jesus says we must be ready to deny ourselves, take up his cross or cause, and follow him, no matter what. The most interesting thing is, for any of us who have tried to do just that, our life takes on so much more meaning than we ever knew was possible. Rejoice at every opportunity God gives you to serve him, especially when it may require a great sacrifice on your part. The blessing will be more than you can imagine.

G.M.D.

prayer

Gracious God, show us the way that you would have us go. Direct our paths that we may be able to serve you as we seek to understand all it means to serve you at any cost. Your love fills our very being and gives us strength to respond to your call. Thank you for allowing us to be your humble servants. In Christ's name and for his sake. Amen.

SING: "Jesu, Jesu"

When We All Get Together

Matthew 18:15-20

James Moore in his book *Yes Lord, I Have Sinned,* tells of a group of people in a play called *Construction* who find themselves in a place they can't identify and don't know why they are there. One of them notices a pile of building materials but no directions. They all begin to argue over what it is they are supposed to build with these materials. Just then one of them sees another group of people coming toward them in the distance. They begin to wonder whether they are safe or not. They decide to build a wall around themselves to protect themselves. As they are building, a person comes up to them carrying a piece of paper. He stops them from their work and tells them they are building it all wrong. They are supposed to be building a bridge to reach out to the other people, not a wall to keep them out.

Too often, even within our church or our choir, we tend to build walls that keep others out rather than bridges that help them to come in. Sometimes the walls are built over misunderstandings of an individual or a group of individuals. One of the hardest things for us to do is to try to rectify a misunderstanding from our side. Maybe we were even right in our thinking but the other person didn't understand it that way. It's our responsibility, Jesus says, to still try to make things right. It may take several of us working on the problem together to be able to rectify the problem. Sometimes the other party or group, refuses to hear us out. Then we have to let them go. We cannot force someone to understand, but we must always be ready to try to work with each other in the most Christian and caring way possible.

The choir has the greatest opportunity for sharing that kind of Christian friendship for all who come into our fellowship. Don't ever lose that warm reputation for inclusiveness and care and love for each other.

G.M.D.

prayer

Loving Lord, help us to share your love with all those who come into our presence. Help us to be an example to other groups within our church, that they may see the love of Christ in our care and our music we share. Amen.

SING: "Let There Be Light"

Forgiveness Unlimited

Matthew 18:21-35

Two years ago an American family was visiting in Italy when a most horrible thing happened to them. While driving in their car in an unfamiliar area, someone shot at them and killed the son. There was absolutely nothing that made any sense in this whole episode. As heartbroken and upset as the family was at the death of their young son, they decided to give his organs to help others. They felt that their son could then continue to have purpose in his life. Just this past year, the two were responsible for his death were acquitted due to lack of substantial evidence. The family was at the trial and after the verdict came in, were asked how they felt about the verdict. Their response overwhelmed the reporters when they said that the trial had been run fairly and they did not hold angry feelings for the two men. They said that anger could not bring their boy back and they had forgiven the two and found peace with God, knowing their son still lived in others. The whole country of Italy had been changed by the generosity and forgiving nature of these, once strangers, now friends. Organ donation went up 40% after their gift of organs to the Italian people. That is one of the most incredible stories of forgiveness, the kind of forgiveness that Jesus was talking about.

Every Sunday in worship we share the Lord's prayer and ask "forgive us our trespasses (sins) as we forgive those who trespass (sin) against us." I think God is taken off the hook, so to speak, in a lot of the sins we commit, as far as forgiving us, if we ask him to forgive us in the same way we forgive others. We so often do not forgive. Jesus tells us to not count the number of times we are wronged, just to forgive others as you would expect your Heavenly Father to forgive you. This may not come easily for some of us, but with a little practice and conscious effort you will be amazed at how much peace it will bring to your life.

G.M.D.

prayer

Loving and forgiving God, we know that we are not always ready to forgive those around us. Sometimes we hang onto a grudge for a very long time and are unable to even ask you for forgiveness when we know we have failed you. Help us to open our hearts in love and forgiveness to others. Lord help us to be able to let go of any lasting hurt feelings. We seek always to do your will in all our relationships. Be with us in Jesus' name. Amen.

SING: "The Lord's Prayer"

Whose World is This?

Matthew 21:33-46

Jesus is saying to the religious leaders of his day that they have failed to understand who they are in relationship to those over whom they have control. God meant for their leadership to be one of care-giving, of opening God's word to God's people. God sent prophet after prophet to try to help the leaders understand and time after time they refused to listen, and even killed God's messengers. Now the very Son of God has arrived with the message, but still the message falls on deaf ears. God's own son would suffer the same indignities that had been the fate of the prophets, even death. But Jesus assures those who are listening that God will triumph in the end. God will save his people.

God was, God is, God will be. When we begin to look at the amount of time we have to spend in God's world, we can better respond to our own calling. We, too, are called to be care-givers to God's people. When we share our musical talents, we are sharing the Word of God with God's people. Thanks be to God! Before any service we must open ourselves to the Holy Spirit and trust in the Holy Spirit to help us reach those who listen to us. We must hear with our hearts and use our voices to proclaim God's love.

prayer

Great God of the universe, help us to be mindful of who you are and whose we are. Remind us each time we lead in worship that we are your servants, your messengers. Help us to reflect your glory in all we say and do. Help us to share your love with those who do not yet know you. As the world comes together in communion today, may we respond to your love in Christ's death and resurrection as one people under your almighty power and love. In Christ's name we pray. Amen.

SING: "Christ for the World We Sing"

Great Christian Fellowship

Matthew 22:1-14

When I went to high school in upstate New York, most of my friends were second generation Italians. Their families, communities, and churches had a great many wonderful festivities and I was often invited to share in the celebrations. Since I lived fifteen miles away, it was hard to accept the invitations very often, but when I could, what great experiences! Nearly all their festivities revolved around their faith in some way—baptism, first communion, weddings, even wakes before a funeral—everything was a big celebration for them. There was always food enough to feed an army, music, dancing, and wonderful fellowship. Having come from a rather conservative religious background, it took some getting used to for this new way to respond to the festivals of the church. It was great!

Jesus is talking about a similar type of celebration. This is the wedding reception for God's son Jesus Christ and we are all invited. Too often we think that to be religious is to be staid and proper to the point of being stuffy. Jesus tells us that there is nothing more joyful or rewarding than sharing with other Christians on special occasions.

During my years of church service I have had many opportunities to share meals with different groups of church leaders. It is a great way to get to know others better and to thank them for their work. Every Sunday we, as the choir, have the opportunity to lead the Lord's celebration. We should have times, too, when we meet to refresh ourselves, to get to know others better, and to celebrate ourselves.

G.M.D.

prayer

Loving God, we thank you for so many blessings and opportunities to share those blessings with your people. Help us to always share the joy of your love with others so that they too may sense the joy of your presence. Guide us in your work so that we may be ready as faithful servants when you call us to your banquet. In Jesus' name we pray. Amen.

SING: "How Great Thou Art"

Like Parent, Like Child

Matthew 22:15-22

I was blessed to have grown up with parents and grandparents who knew and loved the Lord and showed that love through their service to the church and to those around them. Even though I felt "out of sink" because of my frivolous personality, I knew and understood what Christian love was all about. We were also taught the importance of other peoples' positions, paying our bills in a timely manner, giving the right amount of taxes to the government as required, and so on; all the regulations that make for peaceful, correct living both for God and for the state. My family always tithed to the work of the church as well as giving over and beyond that amount when the need was there. There were six children in my family and we were anything but rich, but we still tried to give to those less fortunate than ourselves. When I became an adult, and especially when I was a single parent of five children, all the lessons I had learned as a child remained with me. I had very little but I was always willing to share whatever I had. If I didn't have money for the church I would give extra time to make up for it. Those around us are influenced by the way we live our lives.

Jesus had no problem giving the Roman state its due. Honoring the rights of the state does not take away from our Christian life. Everything we have and all that we are comes from the Lord God first. To live peaceably and in good harmony with our nation requires us to give proportionally to the government of the nation. We do not give to one and not the other, but to both as is appropriate.

God has blessed you with many gifts and talents. Don't be afraid to share them proportionally back to the Lord. We give our sales and income taxes to the working of the government, and we give our lives and all that we are to the work of the Lord.

G.M.D.

prayer

Great God, we thank you for all our gifts and talents and pray that we may always understand how to use all that we are to your glory and honor. Help us to realize that we have all been given different gifts and graces, but that when we seek your will, you will show us how to use these gifts and graces for the work of your church and world. Bless us now with your presence as we seek to serve you in Christ's name. Amen.

An Ancient Formula for a Modern Chorus

Matthew 22:34-46

When I was young and attended church with my parents, every Sunday we heard the reading of the Great Commandments. This was a summary for the reading of the Ten Commandments and quoted Jesus from verses 37-40 of our scripture. I have since learned that the first commandment Jesus noted was and continues to be the opening of worship in Jewish synagogues and temples to this day. Recently, in playing the part of a rabbi, I quoted these words in their Hebrew form: "Shema, Israel, adornai elohim ehad." To quote even these few ancient words can be a very moving experience.

Over the years I have thought about a musical application of the attributes we are called to dedicate to God, especially as found in Mark's version of this incident (Mark 12). Quite aside from the involvement of our total being, it can serve as a formula for our preparation of music for worship. We come to our practices opening our hearts in love for God, for one another, and for music. As we work on a piece, our soul, the innermost part of our being, becomes engaged by the text and the musical setting. Our soul and heart come together in discovering and expressing the sense of the music. Involving our mind in this process, we read the notated music and attend to the relationships of our various parts, harmonies, counterpoints, and movements of tone and rhythm. Our mind informs the discoveries and expressions noted by our soul and heart. Finally, our strength, the physical act of singing and playing, brings all our discoveries, expressions and intellectual observations into a world of sound that must bless all those who hear us.

If we are lacking in one or another aspect of all this, we will miss part of the full spiritual blessing available to ourselves and others. The total love of God must be our aim in all our service of worship. Further, the music chosen for our worship must be able to bear up under such a total demand. It need not be difficult, but it must be sincere, well-crafted, and have some touch of originality to demand and support our emotional, spiritual, mental, and physical selves in our service to God and the people we seek to lead in worship.

H.W.D.

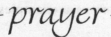

prayer

SING: "When in Our Music God is Glorified"

Some Qualities of a Saint

Matthew 5:1-12

We all have special people in our lives who have made a lasting impression of how we live. They become our saints. The one who is at the top of my list is my fraternal grandmother. My grandfather died before I was born, so I never knew him. After his death, my grandmother lived on a farm in the mountains of Vermont. Three of her children never married and stayed on the farm with her. Four other children did marry and gave her nineteen grandchildren. We were only able to spend a few short days with her each year. When I was in high school, I got to spend two summers helping her with the boarders she took in. It was during those summers that I became aware of how special she really was; she was always even-tempered and at peace with everyone. She had a wonderful way of showing God's love as she cared for the people who entered her home. Her patience with her many grandchildren was without bounds. She was never too busy for us. She truly was a saint.

Fanny Crosby also had a grandmother who shared God's love. One day she said to Fanny, "Will you be with me in God's holy kingdom?" This was a turning point in young Fanny's life. She began living in God's kingdom then and through her songs and singing she led many others to God. She truly was a saint.

Jesus is speaking of people like my grandmother, and Fanny's grandmother. They really understood what it means to be humble, meek, pure in heart, a peacemaker, and to seek God's presence. Jesus was talking about a way of life. Then Jesus goes on to tell of the blessings we will receive when we choose to follow his way.

Let us seek to know God more each day. Let us begin living in God's kingdom now and sharing God's love with all we meet. We have the means through our music to offer Christ to the congregation each week. Our prayer should always be that through our service God will be glorified and others will draw nearer to God.

G.M.D.

prayer

Gracious and loving God, we come before you seeking to know you more and more each day. May the lives we live here on earth be such that those who know us may see your love in us. Help us to be mindful of your presence in all we say and do. Thank you for those who have gone before us as examples of your love. In Jesus' name we pray. Amen.

SING: "Rejoice in God's Saints"

Being Prepared is Always Part of the Plan

Matthew 25:1-13

As I was about to begin this devotion, I noticed that the air from the register seemed very cold. My husband went up to check the gage on the fuel tank and to our amazement, the gauge read completely empty. It has been only a month since we filled this tank that holds three hundred gallons of fuel. Fortunately for us, the temperature is not as cold as it has been these last few weeks. We sure didn't expect to run out this fast. Just like the maidens who were not able to borrow from the other maidens who had enough oil, we cannot get our tank filled until tomorrow. If it gets very cold it will seem too late. Everything we do in life requires some kind of preparation.

Sometime back, one of our astronauts was asked before a moon mission, "What's the most dangerous part of this flight?" He answered, "That part which we have overlooked in our preparations." Preparation is often the difference between success and failure in any project we seek to undertake. As a part of the public worship service in the church, we understand how important it is to be prepared with our part of the service. Sometimes the preparation of an anthem takes only a little practice, but sometimes it takes several weeks to prepare it to the quality we want.

Jesus is talking about a much more profound kind of preparation that is being prepared for his coming. Since none of us have any idea when he will return or when we might see him face to face, it is important to be ready all the time. No matter where we are, what we are doing, or who we are with, we need to be ready for the Lord's coming, or be really left out in the cold.

G.M.D.

prayer

Gracious God, in our busy world we sometimes forget to take the time to do all the things you would have us do. We often overlook the needs of others and we sometimes forget to seek your guiding power in our daily lives. Help us O God, to be more in keeping with your will, Help us to always be ready for your coming again in Jesus Christ to receive us into your heavenly kingdom. We pray always in your Son's holy name. Amen.

SING: "Wake, Awake, for Night is Flying"

Talents: Boon or Bane

Matthew 25:14-30

In our time we have great gifts and resources available to enhance our lives. Jesus' parable of the talents did not solely refer to abilities or even spiritual gifts, but to all our resources. Knowing that we in our church choir are probably all doing our best to maximize our musical gift and provide a blessing for others, let's consider that broader aspect of this parable. In doing so, we may also make some connections to our musical abilities and opportunities in the church.

The things that pass through our household can be seen as gifts of God's creation and God's blessings through human imagination and ingenuity. The use of these gifts to make life less rigorous can give us the opportunity to be blessed and to bless others, if we will use it. Looking to the present, we can take the time made available by work-saving appliances and packaged foods to share meaningfully with our family, church, or community. Or, we can bury that time by working longer to amass a personal fortune, spending time seeking greater physical strength or health for its own sake, or accumulating entertainment experiences in and out of our home.

Looking to the future, some of the resources that pass through our household can be passed back via a recycling program into the great pool of what God gives us. Have you ever noticed how much time it takes, however, to collect and stack newspapers, cut and flatten boxes, rinse out bottles and cans, and to sort your materials for recycling? You have to be committed to make it work! While we may tend to say we trust God's grace and human ingenuity to provide resources for the future, if we fail to recycle we may again be literally burying our talent, a talent-resource that may come into short supply in the future.

If we truly believe that all we have and are comes from God, whether more or less, the parable illustrates our obligation to make appropriate and beneficial use of all our resources. It is interesting to note that, although the ultimate reward comes at the last judgment, the multiplication of the resources occurs during our lifetime. We know from this that blessings we receive from wise use of our talents can be known in the here and now when we continue to work for Christ and God's people.

H.W.D.

prayer

Gracious God, you have been so openhanded with your gifts and benefits to us. Help us to be able and willing to use them for the benefit of others and the greater glory of thy Kingdom. Forgive us when we fail to see opportunities to work for you. Help us never to be so afraid of your requirements that we fail to venture that which can benefit and bless us all. Amen.

SING: "Be Thou My Vision"

What Motivates You?

Matthew 25:31-46

We probably all have heard the anecdote concerning the mountain climbers who ascended Mt. Everest "because it was there." A few outstanding sports figures have been quoted as saying that they would compete no matter what because they just enjoy the competition. We have heard writers, poets, and musical composers say that their works come from some inner compulsion that they cannot resist. So too with the upright in Jesus' parable of the last judgment. They did good without thinking about a reward and seem astonished that anyone, let alone the King of Creation, would have noticed. Theirs was a life of good to "the least of those who are members of my family" simply because it seemed to them the only way to live. Someone has said that they had in them the heart and mind of Jesus. They are the people of the Peaceable Kingdom foretold by Old Testament prophets.

On the other hand, we have all been disgusted by people whose lives appear to be dedicated to fame and fortune. Recall the sports announcers at the most recent Olympic Games pointing out the financial gain awaiting medal holders, and the upset athletes who felt that their sport losses now would ruin them because of a very substantial income loss. One might even question the practice of naming additions or rooms in our church complexes for some significant donor, or even placing a plaque listing the names of donors for the latest addition. Do we really need awards to recognize people for regular church or Sunday school attendance, or to keep choir members coming back into the loft from week to week?

Certainly, various expressions of gratitude and memorials are appropriate, for gratitude to and support for one another is also implied in the King's judgments. If, however, our entire life is lived as though the commandments of the Lord were written on our heart, we would all be astonished by what can be accomplished as well as by the rewards. And the least of Christ's family, our companions in faith, will be the first to benefit from our life of love.

H.W.D.

---

prayer

Our Heavenly Lord and Savior, you give us examples of how our life is to be lived. Help us in our caring and support for one another and others to work and not look for reward and to love without conditions. We would write your law on our hearts and always serve you as sovereign king of the universe. Help us to recognize your kingdom in the unexpected compliment and to spread your love in all our living, Amen.

SING: "When the Poor Ones"

Birthday Celebration

Psalm 92:1-15

Adlai Stevenson used to share this favorite story of an elderly friend who was 102 years old. The elderly gentlemen was being interviewed on his birthday and asked to what he attributed his long life. He replied he had never smoked, drank, nor over-loaded his stomach. He went to bed early and got up early. The reporter said, "You know, I had an uncle who did the same things, but he lived to be only 89. What do you attribute that to?" The old gentleman replied, "He just didn't keep it up long enough." I think most of us tend to quit too soon. Our birthday is a wonderful time to both reminisce about the past and dream about the future while we celebrate the present with family and friends.

The Psalmist has shared with us how wonderful life is when we give our thanks and praise to the Lord. We do not have to think in terms of aging but look always to new and more fulfilling possibilities of who we are as the righteous people of God. The Psalmist uses wonderful descriptive illustrations for the righteous, like palm trees which are known for their long life, and cedar trees which grow up to 120 feet high and 30 feet around. What majestic symbols for those who trust in the Lord all their days. Then he goes on to say that in old age they still produce fruit and they are always green and full of sap, showing that the Lord is upright. What strength is found in his words. What a joyful life awaits those who trust in the Lord. Rejoice in all that life means today, tomorrow and always for those who live in the Lord.

Let me share a quote from Eleanor Roosevelt: "A mature person is one who does not think in absolutes, who is able to be objective even when deeply stirred emotionally, who has learned that there is both good and bad in all people and in all things, and who walks humbly and deals charitably with the circumstances of life, knowing that in this world no one is all-knowing and therefore all of us need both love and charity."

G.M.D.

prayer

Gracious God, we thank you for all that life has in store for us from year to year. We are grateful that you are always with us to guide us and encourage us as we seek to live our lives in a way that will reflect your love to others. We ask a special blessing for (name/s) on this day, that they may feel your presence surrounding them in love. Be with us all, now and always, in Jesus' name. Amen.

SING: (along with "Happy Birthday") "Seek Ye First"

United We Praise

Choir Outing/Retreat

Rather than attempt a typical meditation for such an event as you have at this time, allow us to set a mood and direction by emphasizing some important values that should come out of your activities with the following psalms, hymns, and prayer. Our personal prayer is that God will bless your work together, wherever you are, and that this special time may also come to bless those whom you lead in worship.

READ RESPONSIVELY—Psalm 133:
Behold, how good and pleasant it is
    when we live together in unity!
IT IS LIKE THE PRECIOUS OIL UPON THE HEAD,
    RUNNING DOWN UPON THE BEARD,
UPON THE BEARD OF AARON,
    RUNNING DOWN ON THE COLLAR OF HIS ROBES!
it is like the dew of Hermon
    which falls on the mountains of Zion!
FOR THERE THE LORD HAS COMMANDED THE BLESSING,
    LIFE FOR EVERMORE.

Hymn: "Blest Be the Tie That Binds"

> Blest Be the Tie That Binds
>   our hearts in Christian love;
> the fellowship of kindred minds
>   is like to that above.

> Before our Father's throne
>   we pour our ardent prayers;
> our fears, our hopes, our aims are one,
>   our comforts and our fears.

John Fawcett

READ RESPONSIVELY—Psalm 134:
Come, bless the Lord, all you servants of the Lord,
    WHO STAND BY NIGHT IN THE HOUSE OF THE LORD!
Lift up your hands in the holy place,
    and bless the Lord!
MAY THE LORD WHO MADE HEAVEN AND EARTH
    BLESS YOU FROM ZION.

HYMN: "Stand Up and Bless the Lord"

> Stand Up and Bless the Lord,
>   ye people of his choice;
> stand up and bless the Lord your God
>   with heart and soul and voice.
>
> Stand up and bless the Lord:
>   the Lord your God adore;
> stand up and bless his glorious name,
>   henceforth forevermore.

James Montgomery

PRAY TOGETHER: "For True Singing"

> Glorious God, source of joy and righteousness,
> enable us as redeemed and forgiven children
>   evermore to rejoice in singing your praises.
> Grand that what we sing with our lips
>   we may believe in our hearts,
> and what we believe in our hearts
>   we may practice in our lives;
> so that being doers of the Word and nor hearers only,
>   we may receive everlasting life;
> through Jesus Christ our Lord. Amen.

Fred D. Gealy, USA, 20th cent.; alt. by Laurence Hull Stookey, 1987 Alt. © 1989 The United Methodist Publishing House. Used by permission.

CPSIA information can be obtained
at www.ICGtesting.com
Printed in the USA
LVHW030444120623
749498LV00023B/371